DEC   2016

A BEACON · BIOGRAPHY

Maria von Trapp
and the
Trapp Family Singers

Amy Tiehel

PURPLE TOAD
PUBLISHING

PURPLE TOAD
PUBLISHING

Printing   1   2   3   4   5   6   7   8   9

A Beacon Biography

Angelina Jolie
Big Time Rush
Cam Newton
Carly Rae Jepsen
Daisy Ridley
Drake
Ed Sheeran
Ellen DeGeneres
Elon Musk
Harry Styles of One Direction
Jennifer Lawrence
John Boyega
Kevin Durant
Lorde
Malala
Maria von Trapp
Markus "Notch" Persson, Creator of Minecraft
Mo'ne Davis
Muhammad Ali
Neil deGrasse Tyson
Peyton Manning
Robert Griffin III (RG3)

Publisher's Cataloging-in-Publication Data
Tiehel, Amy.
   Maria von Trapp / written by Amy Tiehel.
      p. cm.
Includes bibliographic references, glossary, and index.
ISBN 9781624692581
1. Trapp, Maria Augusta—Juvenile literature. 2. Folk singers—Biography—Juvenile literature. I. Series: Beacon biography.
   ML3930.T7 2017
   927.8

Library of Congress Control Number: 2016940955

eBook ISBN: 9781624692598

ABOUT THE AUTHOR: Amy Tiehel is the author of Purple Toad's *Long Ago and Far Away: Ancient Egypt*. She has been intrigued with Maria von Trapp's story since the first time she saw *The Sound of Music* as a child. This book combines her love of writing with her joy of learning about one of her childhood heroines. Amy lives near Philadelphia, Pennsylvania.

PUBLISHER'S NOTE: This book is an unauthorized biography.

CONTENTS

A Family
Escapes

German dictator Adolph Hitler arrives in Austria in March 1938. The Anschluss was the "takeover" of Austria by Germany.

On March 11, 1938, Maria von Trapp, her husband Georg, and their nine children heard an announcement on the radio. Their country had been taken over by the German army, led by dictator Adolf Hitler. Maria and her family knew they had to leave their home in Salzburg, Austria. Big red flags with the black Nazi symbol, the swastika, were hanging on buildings. People were expected to say the Nazi greeting, "Heil, Hitler!" to each other.

Soon after, Maria and Georg were touring an art museum called the House of German Art in Munich, Germany. In the museum restaurant, their waiter pointed out Adolf Hitler sitting at the table next to them. He called him *Führer*, which is German for "leader." Maria found him to be "ordinary, a little vulgar and not too well educated."[1] Afterward, she and Georg walked in the colorful gardens outside. Georg remembered a letter he had in his pocket. It was a letter from the German navy.

Georg had been a decorated naval captain in World War I, fighting for the Austro-Hungarian Empire. Now Hitler was commanding him to be a submarine captain in his navy. Georg had already experienced how brutal war could be, but he knew Hitler's army was even more horrifying. Georg did not want to be a part of Hitler's regime. He also did not want to fly the Nazi flag on his home or say, "Heil, Hitler."

Georg von Trapp on the bridge of the SM U 5, the submarine he commanded, 1915

The von Trapp family had become famous for their singing in Austria. Now they were invited to sing at Hitler's birthday party. The concert would make them rich and even more famous. On the other hand, if they refused, they knew their lives could be in danger. Georg explained to the children they could stay and do what the Nazis wanted while keeping the comforts of their home, or they could refuse and keep their faith in God. If they refused, they would have to leave the home they loved.

Maria wrote, "There was no real question what God wanted. As a family it was decided that we wanted to keep *Him*. We understood this meant we had to get out."[2]

In the movie based on Maria's life, *The Sound of Music*, the von Trapps run away from the Nazis in the middle of the night. They hike over the mountains, the Alps, to get to freedom in Switzerland. But that is not what happened in real life. "Don't they know geography in Hollywood? Salzburg does not border on Switzerland!" Maria told a reporter in 1967.[3] In fact, if they had climbed over the Alps from their home, they would have ended up in Germany.

Map of Austria. The von Trapp family lived in Salzburg.

The real story is that the family often went hiking in the Alps. Their neighbors were used to seeing them in their hiking clothes, walking to the train that took them into the mountains. For their escape, the von Trapps pretended they were going hiking, as usual. Carrying only one bag each, they rode a train to Italy. The very next day, the Nazis closed the borders in and out of Austria. The family had gotten out just in time.

Overnight, the von Trapps had become refugees. Maria said, "We went from being rich to being the poorest of poor."[4] They had no money, and their only belongings were the few things they had packed. Maria and Georg had to

German and Austrian soldiers take down a border post, which had separated Austria from Germany, after the German takeover.

figure out a way to make money in order to feed their large family. To complicate their situation, Maria was pregnant.

Before the family left Austria, Georg had written a letter to an American music producer, Mr. Wagner. They hoped he would hire them to sing in America. While the family waited for Mr. Wagner to reply, they performed concerts across Europe. Weeks later, tickets arrived from Mr. Wagner for the whole family to travel to America for a music tour. In October of 1938, the von Trapps boarded the ship the *American Farmer* and left for America.

Maria's determination to keep her family safe and her teamwork with Georg helped her family escape the Nazis. Her strong will and faith in God would continue to help her and her family in the years to come.

As a third grader, Maria received her first communion and promised she would never offend God.

From Orphan to Nun

Maria Augusta Kutschera was born on January 26, 1905, on a train traveling between Tyrol and Vienna, Austria. Her parents were Augusta and Karl Kutschera. Karl was an engineer from Vienna. He spoke fourteen languages and was a skilled musician and devoted reader.

Maria's father was married before he met Maria's mother. Sadly, his first wife died in a horse-drawn carriage accident. Maria's father often visited his first wife's grave. There he met a beautiful woman named Augusta Rainer, called Gusti. She would become his second wife and Maria's mother.

When Maria was two years old, her mother caught pneumonia and also died. Her father was heartbroken and felt he could not take care of Maria. He left her with his cousin, who became Maria's foster mother. They lived on a farm in the small town of Kagran, outside of Vienna.

Maria spent her days gathering vegetables from neighboring farms, collecting water at the city spring in the nearby Vienna Woods, and attending school. Her foster mother was a religious person and shared Bible stories with her. In this gentle and loving way, God entered Maria's life.[1] Her foster mother would tell her: "God is everywhere and sees you always."[2]

The Austrian town of Tyrol, where Maria lived as a child before her mother died.

After some time, Maria was reunited with her father. She enjoyed visiting him in his apartment in Vienna. He had one room full of birds of all colors. Maria loved looking at them and listening to them tweet. But when she was nine her father died, too, and that was the end of her childhood.[3]

Now she was an orphan and everything changed. Her Uncle Franz became her guardian. The comforting, carefree life she had known on her foster mother's farm was gone, because Uncle Franz was strict and abusive. He was also a socialist, and believed religion was used to control people. Maria was no longer allowed to discuss religion. The Bible stories she loved, she recalled, were "branded as silly legends without a word of truth."[4] Maria felt an inner emptiness and missed her connection with God.

One day Maria realized that no matter what she said or did, Uncle Franz would find a reason to beat her. She changed from a quiet, shy girl into an outspoken, social girl. She got in trouble at school. But she enjoyed reading like her father, so she passed her classes and graduated.

The resort town of Semmering, Austria was a safe haven for Maria, far from her Uncle Franz.

After graduation Maria wanted to go to the State Teacher's College. Uncle Franz would not give her the money to go. She decided to make the money on her own, and ran away with her friend Annie to the resort town of Semmering, Austria. There she taught children who were staying in the fancy resort hotels. After a summer of hard work, Maria had enough money to pay for college.

The renowned Vienna Boy's Choir was a favorite of Maria's. She listened to them at the Chapel of the Imperial Palace on Sundays.

She entered the State Teacher's College of Progressive Education in Vienna that September. She admitted she was "always hungry for music and in Vienna there was always music."[5] In church, she could listen to the Vienna Philharmonic or to the Vienna Boys' Choir.

One Palm Sunday, Maria attended church hoping to hear more music. Instead she heard a Jesuit priest give a powerful sermon about Jesus Christ.

As she recalled, "The way this man talked just swept me off of my feet."[6] His sermon made Maria doubt what Uncle Franz had taught her about the Bible being untrue. She spoke to the priest, who pronounced, "Thy sins are forgiven." Then Maria accepted God back into her life.

Maria was so grateful to be forgiven that she wanted to give back to God. On a hiking trip in the mountains, as she would later write, she "spread her arms wide and shouted, 'Thank You, God, for this great wonderful creation of Yours. What could I give You back for it?'"[6] She realized the way to give back to God would be to give up all that she loved in nature and commit herself to God in a convent.

Maria walked right off the mountain and into the Benedictine Abbey of Nonnberg. She spent the next year at the abbey, teaching fifth grade and trying her best to obey the rules.

Nonnberg Abbey was founded in the year 714. It was known as one of the strictest abbeys in Salzburg.

Maria was a novitiate, which is a person soon to take the final vows to become a nun. Novitiates were not allowed to whistle, talk, run through the abbey, or argue with a superior. Maria often broke these rules.

In her second year at the abbey, the Reverend Mother called Maria to her office. Maria thought she was in trouble as usual, but that was not the reason for the meeting. The Reverend Mother explained that a Captain von Trapp had a daughter who was sick. This daughter, also named Maria, had scarlet fever and needed a teacher.

Maria was happy at the abbey, and she pleaded with the Reverend Mother to let her stay. But the Reverend Mother said it was God's will that she go.

After living behind the protective gates of Nonnberg Abbey for two years, Maria left for a new life with the von Trapp family.

Young Maria had only the dress and hat she wore, a small bag, and her guitar when she arrived at the von Trapp family villa.

Maria Marries the Captain

In 1926, Maria left her simple life at the abbey for the von Trapp family villa. The home included a large mansion with many beautiful rooms, surrounded by gardens, flowers, and trees. She was there to teach eleven-year-old Maria, but soon she fell in love with all seven of the von Trapp children: Rupert, Werner, Johanna, Agathe, Maria, Martina, and Hedwig. Their father, Captain Georg von Trapp, was kind and loved his children very much, but he was often away.

Maria taught the younger children, but the older children would also stop to listen when they were bored. One rainy Saturday, Werner noticed the guitar that Maria had on her wall. He asked if she could play it. Maria said she could and taught them all the Austrian folk songs and Christmas songs she knew. After that they spent the evenings sitting in front of a cozy fire, telling stories and singing the songs they learned. Captain von Trapp played the violin, and he joined in the singing whenever he was home. Maria finally felt all the love that she had missed as a child. She remembered, "Suddenly Martina crawled on my lap, hugging me tight, and covered my face with kisses."[1]

Maria fell into a happy routine at the von Trapp villa. Even so, she missed the convent and thought about going back. But God had other plans for her.

At age 22, Maria married Baron Georg von Trapp. The whole town came to the wedding.

Captain von Trapp asked Maria to marry him and become the mother to his children.

Maria was not in love with Georg, but she loved the children very much. She said, "If he had only asked me to marry him I might not have said yes. . . . [H]owever, I loved the children, and so in a way I really married the children."[2] Georg and Maria were married on November 26, 1927, and in time Maria truly fell in love with Georg.

Fifteen months later, on February 28, 1929, Maria gave birth to their first child, Rosemarie. Two years after that another daughter, Eleonore, was born. Maria was content and her life was full. She enjoyed running the large house, raising her stepchildren and daughters, and being a wife.

At the same time, a dark cloud was hovering over Germany as the dictator Adolf Hitler and his Nazi party gained power. Hitler closed the Austrian border to Germans, and tourism stopped. The bank where Georg kept his money failed, and he lost most of his money.

Always determined and hardworking, Maria kept the family going by renting the rooms in their large home. She took in students from the nearby Catholic University, as well as a young priest, Father Wasner. The director of Gregorian chants at the seminary, Father Wasner had come to say mass at the villa in 1935. When he heard the von Trapps sing, he was very impressed. He signed on as their musical director. Under his guidance the family developed from amateur singers into professionals. They called themselves the Trapp Family Choir.

A year later, Maria and the children were singing in the garden when they heard someone clapping. On the other side of

Father Wasner (seated, right) rehearses with the von Trapp Family singers. Maria is on the far right.

the fence was the famous opera singer Lotte Lehmann, who had been walking by their home. Impressed, she insisted they appear the very next day at the popular Austrian music festival in Salzburg.

Lotte Lehmann, famous German soprano, discovered the von Trapp family singers.

The Trapp Family Choir entered the festival and won! After the festival they had many invitations to sing. They had offers from music managers around the world, including the United States. Maria and the family toured Europe, performing for kings and queens and even Pope Pius XI.

When Austria fell to Hitler in 1938, Maria wrote, "Our cheerful house of song had become a house of mourning."[3] She and her family escaped to Italy, and then sailed to the United States.

The von Trapp family on tour, smiling for the camera in 1939. Left to right, top: Werner and Rupert; middle: Dr. Franz Wasner, Martina, Maria (holding baby Johannes), Captain von Trapp, Johanna, Hedwig, daughter Maria; bottom: Agatha, Rosemarie, and Eleanore.

Chapter 4

The Trapp Family Singers

During the voyage across the Atlantic, Maria realized she was going to have to learn English. Determined as always, she said, " 'All right. If I have to learn English, let's go!' "[1] Pointing to her watch, she asked the American passengers what the English word was, and in this way she began to learn the language.

The von Trapp family arrived in New York City in the autumn of 1938. At first, adjusting to their new country was hard. Everything seemed so big, noisy, and different. Slowly they grew used to their life in America. They began their singing tour of the country on a big bus. Their friendly driver took the time to explain American customs, and he would honk the horn whenever they crossed a new state line.

After months of touring, a friend helped Maria and the family find a home to rent near Philadelphia, Pennsylvania. Soon after, on January 17, 1939, Maria gave birth to her third child, Johannes.

For the next fifteen years Maria and her family gave concerts all over their new country and the world. Along the way they changed their name from the Trapp Family Choir to the Trapp Family Singers. The family was often broke, but Maria always put her faith in God that everything would work out—and it did.

Maria and Georg loved their farm in Vermont and the view of the mountains.

During one of these tours they stopped in Stowe, Vermont. The family loved the town because the mountains there reminded them of the Alps in Austria. In 1942, they bought a 660-acre farm. The old building on the property collapsed, so Maria and the whole family built a house. It had been so hard for the von Trapps to leave their homeland of Austria. Now they had a place to call their own in America, where they could gather around the fire just as they had done before.

In 1944, Maria had the idea to start a music camp on the farm. Named the Trapp Family Music Camp, it introduced music to American families. The von Trapps ran the camp when they were not on tour. It became very popular and successful.

While they were touring and busy with the music camp, Georg was diagnosed with cancer. He died in 1947, and Maria was devastated. Georg was buried next to their home. Maria sat on the bench by his grave every day and talked to him. She found peace knowing that her Georg was with God.

Around this time, the von Trapps received a letter explaining that people in Austria were suffering after World War II. Maria and the children decided to create a charity called the Trapp Family Austrian Relief. While they toured, they asked people to donate money and clothing to this cause. Maria would explain, "Few people can imagine what is happening in Austria, whose citizens are about to lose courage and hope."[2] She was later awarded the Benemerenti medal from Pope Pius XII for the help the family provided.

In 1949, Maria wrote her memoir, *The Story of the Trapp Family Singers*. She didn't know it then, but this book would inspire a Broadway musical and Hollywood film called *The Sound of Music*. In 1952, she wrote *Yesterday, Today and Forever*. This book detailed her deep commitment to God and her spiritual life.

In 1955 the Trapp Family Singers held their last concert in The Town Hall in the heart of New York City. They had spent years singing around the world, connecting with people through their music. Now their touring days were over and Maria wondered, *what next*?

Maria sings with her children in London, England 1950.

Christopher Plummer played Captain von Trapp and Julie Andrews played Maria in the 1965 film **The Sound of Music.**

The Sound of Music

On their final world tour, the Trapp Family Singers had stopped in Australia. While there, Maria was invited to visit the South Seas (Oceania) as a missionary. Missionaries travel to other countries to teach Christianity. In 1956, Maria, Father Wasner, and three of the von Trapp children (Maria, Rosemarie, and Johannes) traveled through the islands of New Guinea, visiting the people and teaching them the Bible.

While she was doing her missionary work, Maria received letters from music producers. They wanted to make her book, *The Story of the Trapp Family Singers*, into a musical. The musical would star the actress Mary Martin as Maria. Maria said, "I didn't even know who Mary Martin was ... . I went back into the jungle for much more interesting and worthwhile work."[1]

When Maria returned from New Guinea, the theater producers convinced her that they really did want to create a play based on her book. Mary Martin would play her in a musical version of her life. *The Sound of Music* became a huge Broadway success. In 1965 the musical was adapted to film, starring Julie Andrews. It became one of the highest grossing films ever and won five Academy Awards, including Best Picture of the Year. The film is so popular that in 1998, the family received medals of honor from the Salzburg government because the movie had greatly increased tourism there.[2]

Theodore Bikel as Georg and Mary Martin as Maria in the stage production of The Sound of Music

After she had written her book, Maria signed away most of her rights to it. As a result, she didn't have much say over how her life story was adapted. The movie was different from the real von Trapp story. In the movie Captain von Trapp is portrayed as detached and cold-hearted, but Johannes von Trapp said his father was "a very charming man, generous, open, and not the martinet he was made out to be both in the stage play and in the film."[3] Also, Maria did not teach the von Trapp children how to sing. They already enjoyed singing before Maria arrived. She taught them more songs, and then Father Wasner organized them into a professional singing group.

Maria and the von Trapp family did not receive a lot of money, despite the massive success of the musical and the film. As always, Maria turned to her faith, finding a different sort of reward. She wrote, "There is the uncountable number of letters from all countries of the world, telling me that looking at the film . . . has strengthened their trust in God. Letters like

Rodgers and Hammerstein's indelible music has helped propel the film to number three on the all-time U.S. box office sales (adjusted for inflation). It ranks just below Gone with the Wind and Star Wars.

this make me fold my hands and say . . . Dear Lord, thank You for *The Sound of Music*."[4]

After *The Sound of Music*, Maria was recognized everywhere she went. She was invited to give speeches around the world. She was invited to the White House, where she met President Lyndon B. Johnson. Maria and Dolores Hope, wife of the famous comedian Bob Hope, became friends. (The Hopes often vacationed at the Trapp Family Lodge.) Maria continued to write, authoring the book *Maria, My Own Story*, published in 1972. Through the 1960s and 1970s, she ran the Trapp Family Lodge, which grew to include a successful gift shop. She also devoted herself to answering the many letters she continued to receive.

On March 28, 1987, at the age of eighty-two, Maria von Trapp died from heart failure. Her son Johannes said, "Maria was a force of nature. . . . It wasn't easy to disagree with her but she kept everything together ... . She was an extraordinarily strong person."[5]

People around the world know Maria von Trapp's story because of *The Sound of Music*. But that is only a small part of her incredible life. She had a difficult childhood as an orphan in Austria, but as an adult sang for kings and queens. She lived the simple life of a nun, then married and raised ten children. She became a refugee and then built a

Maria von Trapp found joy in God, her family, and music.

home and successful lodge in America. Along the way, she was always guided by her faith in God. She said, "There is a certain something about wanting to do the will of God . . . in that silence one will always hear that still small voice in one's heart telling him what to do."[6]

1948 Pope Pius XII honors Maria with Benemerenti Medal for Trapp Family Austrian Relief, Inc., an organization that aided thousands of Austrians during World War II.

1952 Pope Pius XII names Maria a Dame of the Order of the Holy Sepulchre.

1956 She is named Catholic Mother of the Year in the United States.

1957 The Republic of Austria honors her with the Decoration of Honour in Gold for Services to the Republic of Austria.

1962 Theta Phi Alpha women's fraternity gives her the Siena Medal, an award to "an outstanding woman to recognize her for great accomplishment."

1967 She receives the Honorary Cross, First Class, for Science and Art from the Austrian government.

2012 A street in Vienna is named Maria Trapp-Platz.

Books Written by Maria von Trapp

1972 *Maria, My Own Story*

1959 *A Family on Wheels*, with Ruth T. Murdoch

1952 *Yesterday, Today and Forever*

1949 *The Story of The Trapp Family Singers*

1905	Maria Augusta Kutschera is born on January 26 on a train between Tyrol and Vienna, Austria.
1907	Maria's mother, Augusta, dies of pneumonia.
1907	Her father, Karl Kutschera, leaves her with a foster mother.
1914	Maria's father dies. She is left in care of her abusive Uncle Franz.
1920	She graduates from high school and runs away to work in Semmering, a resort town.
1924	She graduates from the State Teachers College of Progressive Education in Vienna.
1924	She converts to Catholicism and joins the Nonnberg Benedictine Convent in Salzburg to become a nun.
1926	Maria is sent from the convent to teach Captain Georg von Trapp's daughter Maria, who is sick and can't attend school.
1927	Maria marries Captain Georg von Trapp on November 26.
1929	Georg and Maria's first child, Rosemarie, is born on February 28.
1931	Their second child, Eleonore, or Lorli, is born on May 14.
1936	The von Trapp family sings in the Salzburg Music Festival, winning the amateur contest. Maria and Father Wasner begin the Trapp Family Choir.
1938	The Nazis take over Austria, and the von Trapp family leaves for America.
1939	Georg and Maria's third child, Johannes, is born. World War II starts, September 1.
1938–1950s	The von Trapp family tours the world singing as the Trapp Family Singers.
1942	The von Trapp family buys a 660-acre farm in Stowe, Vermont.
1944	The first von Trapp Family music camp is held in Stowe.
1947	Georg von Trapp dies on May 30. Trapp Family Austrian Relief, Inc. is founded.
1948	Maria and her family become U.S. citizens. They change their name from von Trapp to Trapp.
1949	Maria's book *The Story of the Trapp Family Singers* is published.
1952	Her book *Yesterday, Today and Forever* is published.
1955	The Trapp Family Singers finish their last tour with a performance in Town Hall in New York.
1956	Maria and her children Johannes and Rosemarie and stepdaughter Maria go to the South Seas with Father Wasner to do missionary work.
1959	The musical *The Sound of Music*, based on Maria's book *The Story of the Trapp Family Singers*, opens on Broadway starring actress Mary Martin. *A Family on Wheels*, written by Maria with Ruth T. Murdoch, is published.
1965	The film version of *The Sound of Music*, starring Julie Andrews as Maria, is released.
1960s–1970s	Maria lectures around the world and runs the Trapp Family Lodge in Stowe, Vermont.
1972	Maria's book *Maria* is published.
1987	On March 28, at age 82, Maria von Trapp dies of heart failure in Morrisville, Vermont. Her children continue to run the Trapp Family Lodge.

CHAPTER NOTES

Chapter 1
1. Trapp, Maria Augusta. *The Story of The Trapp Family Singers,* 1949. Reprint, New York: Harper Perennial, 2002, p. 122.
2. von Trapp, Maria. *Maria, My Own Story.* Creation House Inc, Publishers, 1972, p. 88.
3. Hidalgo, Louise. "The Truth About The Sound of Music Family," *BBC News,* March 1, 2015, http://www.rd.com/culture/sound-of-music-facts/
4. Santopietro, Tom. *The Sound of Music.* New York: St. Martin's Press, 2015, p. 16.

Chapter 2
1. von Trapp, Maria. *Maria, My Own Story.* Creation House Inc, Publishers, 1972, p. 20.
2. Ibid., p. 20.
3. Ibid., p. 34.
4. Ibid., p. 42.
5. Ibid., p. 4
6. Santopietro, Tom. *The Sound of Music.* New York: St. Martin's Press, 2015, p. 11.

Chapter 3
1. von Trapp, Maria. *Maria, My Own Story.* Creation House Inc., Publishers, 1972, p. 76.
2. Ibid., p. 77.
3. Trapp, Maria Augusta. *The Story of The Trapp Family Singers.* 1949. Reprint, New York: Harper Perennial, 2002, p. 116.

Chapter 4
1. Trapp, Maria Augusta. *The Story of The Trapp Family Singers,* 1949. Reprint, New York: Harper Perennial, 2002. p. 129.
2. *The Sound of Music Guide,* http://www.the-sound-of-music-guide.com/maria-von-trapp.html, 2015.

Chapter 5
1. von Trapp, Maria. *Maria, My Own Story.* Creation House Inc, Publishers, 1972, p. 207.
2. Von Trapp Family Website, http://www.trappfamily.com/von-trapp-story.htm
3. Hidalgo, Louise. "The Truth About *The Sound of Music* Family," BBC News, March 1, 2015. http://www.bbc.com/news/magazine-31658799
4. Trapp, Maria, p. 218.
5. Hidalgo.
6. Trapp, p. 99.

Books

Anderson, William (Author), and Linda Graves (Illustrator). *V is for Von Trapp: A Musical Family Alphabet.* Ann Arbor, MI: Sleeping Bear Press, 2010.

Roche, Jess. *Jaw-Dropping Geography: Fun Learning Facts About Awesome Austria: Illustrated Fun Learning for Kids, Volume 1.* North Charleston, SC: CreateSpace Independent Publishing Platform, 2015.

Turner, Daniel. *Simple History: A Simple Guide to World War II.* North Charleston, SC: CreateSpace Independent Publishing Platform, 2015.

On the Internet

14 Things You Might Not Know About The Sound of Music
http://mentalfloss.com/article/61706/14-things-you-might-not-know-about-sound-music

Real Life Sound of Music – Great grandchildren of Maria and Georg von Trapp
http://austin.culturemap.com/news/entertainment/von-trapp-family-singers-make-austin-home/#slide=0

Sound of Music Interactive
http://www.sound-of-music-interactive.com/index.html

Works Consulted

Books

Santopietro, Tom. *The Sound of Music Story.* New York: St. Martin's Press, 2015.

Trapp, Maria Augusta. *Maria, My Own Story.* 1972. Reprint, New York: Avon Books, 1973.

Trapp, Maria Augusta. *The Story of The Trapp Family Singers.* 1949. Reprint, New York: Harper Perennial, 2002.

On the Internet

Gearin, Joan. *"Movie vs. Reality: The Real Story of the von Trapp Family,* Winter 2005. http://www.archives.gov/publications/prologue/2005/winter/von-trapps.html

Hidalgo, Louise. "The Truth About *The Sound of Music Family,"* *BBC News,* March 1, 2015. http://www.bbc.com/news/magazine-31658799

Kerr, Peter. *"Maria von Trapp, 82, Is Dead. Portrayed in Sound of Music."* *The New York Times,* March 30, 1987. http://www.nytimes.com/1987/03/30/obituaries/maria-von-trapp-82-is-dead-portrayed-in-sound-of-music.html

Trapp Family Lodge. "Von Trapp Family Biography." 2016. http://www.trappfamily.com/von-trapp-story.htm

Further Viewing

Movie

The Sound of Music, Director Robert Wise, Performers Julie Andrews as Maria and Christopher Plummer as Georg von Trapp. 20th Century Fox, 1965, Film.

Television

The Sound of Music, NBC, Director Beth McCarthy-Miller, Performers Carrie Underwood as Maria and Stephen Moyer as Captain von Trapp. December 5, 2013, Live Television, and available on DVD.

Documentaries

The Von Trapp Family: Harmony and Discord, 1998, Director Bruce Alfred. Cobblestone Films, 1998, DVD.

Climbed Every Mountain: The Story Behind the Sound of Music, Director Christopher Walker. Zodiak Rights, December 29, 2012, American Public Television.

abbey (AB-ee)—A building or group of buildings where monks or nuns live.

convent (KON-vent)—A place where a group of religious people, usually nuns, live together.

governess (GUH-ver-ness)—A woman who is hired to teach children in their home.

guardian (GAR-dee-un)—A person who looks after someone, particularly a child whose parents have died.

Jesuit (JEH-zoo-it)—A man who is a member of the Roman Catholic Society of Jesus.

martinet (mar-tin-ET)—Someone who is very strict, expecting rules to be followed exactly.

missionary (MISH-uh-nayr-ee)—A person sent on a religious trip, particularly to a foreign country, to teach Christianity.

Nazi (NAHT-zee)—A member of the political party that ruled Germany from 1933 to 1945. Nazis believed in ethnic cleansing (killing people who did not look like or believe in the same things as party members).

novitiate (noh-VIH-shee-it)—A person who is new to a religious group, before he or she takes the vows to be a full member.

Socialist (SOH-shuh-list)—A person who believes in socialism—spreading wealth evenly among all people and treating all people the same.

swastika (SWAH-stih-kuh)—During the twentieth century, the swastika became a symbol of aggression and hatred when it was adopted as the emblem of the Nazi party in Germany.

INDEX